High-Inte Activities in Mathematics

by Gunter Schymkiw

World Teachers Press

Published with the permission of R.I.C. Publications Pty. Ltd.

First published by R.I.C. Publications Pty. Ltd., Perth, Western Australia.

Printed in the United States of America.

Order Number 2-5065
ISBN 1-885111-79-7

A B C D E F 98 99 00 01

395 Main Street
Rowley, MA 01969

Foreword

High-Interest Activities in Mathematics is the third book in the **High-Interest** series, which also includes **High-Interest Activities in Language** and **High-Interest Activities in Vocabulary**. The aim of this series is to provide students with stimulating activities which consolidate essential skills across a number of curriculum areas.

The activities in **High-Interest Mathematics** integrate mathematics with the other key learning areas of English, Human Society, Science and Technology and Creative and Practical Arts. A variety of learning approaches and styles are provided. You can use the book for formal classroom lessons, review and reinforcement, extension work or homework.

It is hoped the activities chosen will enhance students' sense of wonder about the complex, fascinating and relevant nature of the study of mathematics.

Gunter Schymkiw

Table of Contents

Archimedes Cipher

Use the code below to complete the story of the great thinker and inventor, Archimedes.

Code key:
A=1, B=2, C=3, D=4, E=5, F=6, G=7, H=8, I=9, J=10, K=11, L=12, M=13, N=14, O=15, P=16, Q=17, R=18, S=19, T=20, U=21, V=22, W=23, X=24, Y=25, Z=26

Archimedes was a mathematician who lived in ancient **GREECE** (7 18 5 5 3 5) 300 years before Christ was born. He made many **GREAT** (7 18 5 1 20) discoveries but is best known for running naked through the streets of the city Syracuse shouting "Eureka!" which means, "I've **FOUND** (6 15 21 14 4) it!"

He had been at the public **BATHS** (2 1 20 8 19) when he thought of the solution to a problem that his King, **HIERO** (8 9 5 18 15), had asked him to solve. Hiero had employed a **GOLDSMITH** (7 15 12 4 19 13 9 20 8) to make him a crown of pure gold. The **KING** (11 9 14 7) thought that this man had mixed the gold **WITH** (23 9 20 8) another metal. He had kept some of the gold for himself, the king was **QUITE** (17 21 9 20 5) sure. But how could this be proved? Hiero had **GIVEN** (7 9 22 5 14) the man a weight of gold to be **MELTED** (13 5 12 20 5 4) down to make the crown. The crown was made. It **WEIGHED** (23 5 9 7 8 5 4) as much as the original piece of gold. Archimedes knew that any particular weight of gold would have a different **VOLUME** (22 15 12 21 13 5) (i.e., take up a different amount of space) to the same weight of another metal.

What he needed to do was **FIND** (6 9 14 4) the volume of the crown.

As he put his **FOOT** (6 15 15 20) into the bath he saw that the water **OVERFLOWED** (15 22 5 18 6 12 15 23 5 4).

Suddenly he realized that he had **FOUND** (6 15 21 14 4) the answer to the problem! The volume of his foot was the same as the volume of water that had overflowed! His foot had **DISPLACED** (4 9 19 16 12 1 3 5 4) the same volume of water as it occupied itself! If he put the crown into a container filled with water it would displace its own **VOLUME** (22 15 12 21 13 5).

He compared this with the volume displaced by the same weight of pure gold and found that the crown displaced **MORE** (13 15 18 5) water. This meant that the goldsmith had substituted some of the gold for a less valuable metal.

The goldsmith was put to **DEATH** (4 5 1 20 8) by King Hiero.

Which do you think would take up the most space, a kilogram of lead or a kilogram of aluminium?

To complete this mosaic, color the facts with this key.

Mosaic Pattern I

Green 8 · Orange 9 · Yellow 10 · Brown 11 · Blue 12

7 + 2	6 + 3	5 + 4	4 + 5	3 + 6	2 + 7	1 + 8	0 + 9	7 + 2	2 + 7	3 + 6	4 + 5	1 + 11	12 + 0	0 + 12	6 + 6	5 + 7	0 + 12
9 + 0	8 + 1	1 + 9	8 + 1	8 + 2	4 + 5	2 + 8	7 + 2	4 + 6	8 + 1	5 + 5	5 + 4	10 + 2	11 + 1	2 + 10	3 + 9	9 + 3	7 + 5
0 + 9	9 + 0	4 + 5	5 + 4	3 + 6	6 + 3	5 + 4	6 + 3	9 + 0	1 + 8	6 + 3	3 + 6	4 + 7	3 + 8	2 + 9	1 + 10	0 + 11	4 + 8
5 + 4	9 + 1	4 + 5	3 + 6	2 + 7	1 + 8	2 + 9	4 + 7	3 + 8	6 + 5	8 + 3	7 + 3	5 + 6	5 + 5	7 + 4	4 + 6	3 + 8	8 + 4
6 + 3	0 + 10	5 + 4	3 + 6	6 + 3	7 + 2	7 + 4	9 + 2	5 + 6	11 + 0	7 + 4	6 + 4	6 + 5	3 + 7	8 + 3	6 + 4	11 + 0	6 + 6
7 + 2	10 + 0	4 + 5	0 + 9	9 + 0	8 + 1	6 + 3	5 + 4	4 + 5	3 + 6	2 + 7	1 + 8	9 + 0	8 + 1	0 + 9	9 + 2	10 + 1	7 + 5
8 + 1	9 + 0	8 + 1	7 + 2	3 + 7	7 + 2	2 + 8	6 + 3	8 + 2	5 + 4	9 + 1	4 + 5	1 + 9	5 + 4	1 + 8	8 + 4	9 + 3	10 + 2
3 + 5	4 + 4	3 + 6	6 + 3	2 + 7	1 + 8	4 + 5	5 + 4	9 + 0	1 + 8	2 + 7	3 + 6	4 + 5	7 + 2	2 + 7	5 + 7	4 + 8	3 + 9
0 + 9	9 + 0	8 + 1	7 + 2	7 + 3	6 + 3	6 + 4	2 + 7	4 + 6	9 + 0	5 + 5	5 + 4	9 + 1	6 + 3	3 + 6	8 + 3	3 + 8	2 + 10
8 + 1	1 + 8	3 + 6	6 + 3	7 + 2	5 + 4	4 + 5	3 + 6	1 + 8	0 + 9	8 + 1	7 + 2	6 + 3	5 + 4	4 + 5	1 + 9	4 + 7	1 + 11
5 + 4	0 + 10	2 + 7	8 + 3	7 + 4	4 + 7	6 + 5	5 + 6	11 + 0	0 + 11	10 + 1	1 + 10	9 + 2	2 + 9	6 + 5	5 + 6	7 + 4	11 + 1
6 + 3	1 + 9	4 + 5	3 + 8	1 + 11	10 + 2	3 + 9	2 + 10	9 + 3	8 + 4	4 + 8	7 + 5	12 + 0	11 + 1	1 + 11	12 + 0	1 + 11	12 + 0
3 + 6	2 + 8	8 + 1	1 + 8	0 + 9	9 + 0	1 + 8	8 + 1	7 + 2	2 + 7	5 + 7	6 + 6	1 + 11	10 + 2	3 + 9	0 + 12	11 + 1	0 + 12
2 + 7	7 + 2	5 + 4	4 + 5	3 + 7	2 + 7	4 + 6	9 + 0	5 + 5	6 + 3	3 + 6	8 + 4	0 + 12	8 + 4	9 + 3	6 + 6	10 + 2	2 + 10
1 + 8	9 + 0	8 + 1	7 + 2	6 + 3	3 + 6	1 + 8	0 + 9	8 + 1	7 + 2	5 + 6	4 + 7	7 + 4	8 + 3	4 + 8	7 + 5	2 + 10	6 + 6
8 + 1	0 + 9	1 + 8	8 + 1	6 + 3	3 + 6	7 + 2	2 + 7	4 + 7	6 + 4	9 + 2	2 + 9	7 + 3	6 + 5	3 + 8	5 + 7	3 + 9	7 + 5
2 + 7	3 + 6	6 + 3	4 + 5	5 + 4	9 + 0	0 + 9	3 + 6	8 + 3	7 + 4	6 + 5	5 + 6	3 + 8	4 + 8	8 + 4	9 + 3	5 + 7	
4 + 5	5 + 4	6 + 3	3 + 6	7 + 2	2 + 7	1 + 8	6 + 3	1 + 8	4 + 5	5 + 4	4 + 5	2 + 7	5 + 4	5 + 7	7 + 5	8 + 4	4 + 8
5 + 4	2 + 7	4 + 6	6 + 3	3 + 7	8 + 1	2 + 8	7 + 2	1 + 9	3 + 6	0 + 10	7 + 2	8 + 2	1 + 8	3 + 6	6 + 5	5 + 6	8 + 4
6 + 3	3 + 6	5 + 5	8 + 1	7 + 3	1 + 8	9 + 1	2 + 7	3 + 7	5 + 4	7 + 3	9 + 0	9 + 1	0 + 9	4 + 5	6 + 3	7 + 4	4 + 8
7 + 2	2 + 7	6 + 4	1 + 8	8 + 2	9 + 0	10 + 0	4 + 5	6 + 4	6 + 3	4 + 6	6 + 3	10 + 0	8 + 1	3 + 6	8 + 3	4 + 7	5 + 7
3 + 6	6 + 3	5 + 4	4 + 5	9 + 0	0 + 9	7 + 2	5 + 4	8 + 1	2 + 7	7 + 2	3 + 6	2 + 7	4 + 5	10 + 1	9 + 2	3 + 8	7 + 5
4 + 5	5 + 4	1 + 8	0 + 9	1 + 8	10 + 1	9 + 2	8 + 3	7 + 4	6 + 5	5 + 6	4 + 7	3 + 8	11 + 0	0 + 11	1 + 10	2 + 9	6 + 6
8 + 0	2 + 6	9 + 0	8 + 1	2 + 7	11 + 0	7 + 5	8 + 4	9 + 3	10 + 2	11 + 1	12 + 0	0 + 12	1 + 11	2 + 10	3 + 9	4 + 8	5 + 7
4 + 5	5 + 4	2 + 7	7 + 2	3 + 6	5 + 6	6 + 6	5 + 7	4 + 8	3 + 9	2 + 10	1 + 11	12 + 0	4 + 8	5 + 7	7 + 5	6 + 6	8 + 4
3 + 6	6 + 3	8 + 1	9 + 0	4 + 5	5 + 4	6 + 3	7 + 2	8 + 1	9 + 0	0 + 9	1 + 8	2 + 7	3 + 6	4 + 5	5 + 4	2 + 7	4 + 8
2 + 7	7 + 2	7 + 2	4 + 6	6 + 3	5 + 5	3 + 6	4 + 6	1 + 8	3 + 7	9 + 0	2 + 8	0 + 9	1 + 9	8 + 1	0 + 10	1 + 8	6 + 6
1 + 8	0 + 9	9 + 0	8 + 1	7 + 2	6 + 3	5 + 4	4 + 5	3 + 6	2 + 7	1 + 8	0 + 9	9 + 0	8 + 1	7 + 2	6 + 3	7 + 2	5 + 7

Mosaic Pattern II

Grey 10   Brown 11   Yellow 12   Green 14   Blue 13   Red 15

To complete this mosaic, color the facts using the key.

5 + 6	13 + 0	6 + 7	11 + 2	2 + 11	3 + 10	10 + 3	8 + 5	4 + 9	9 + 4	7 + 6	8 + 5	5 + 8	6 + 7
10 + 1	7 + 6	12 + 1	5 + 8	7 + 6	6 + 7	5 + 8	2 + 11	11 + 2	12 + 1	1 + 12	0 + 13	13 + 0	7 + 6
6 + 5	1 + 12	0 + 13	4 + 10	5 + 9	9 + 5	8 + 5	3 + 10	10 + 3	4 + 9	9 + 4	8 + 5	5 + 8	10 + 3
0 + 11	7 + 3	5 + 5	4 + 6	10 + 4	8 + 6	9 + 4	4 + 9	10 + 3	3 + 10	4 + 9	6 + 7	2 + 11	11 + 2
7 + 4	8 + 2	4 + 8	3 + 7	2 + 12	3 + 11	5 + 7	8 + 4	8 + 6	2 + 11	9 + 4	4 + 9	7 + 6	3 + 10
6 + 5	6 + 4	1 + 9	2 + 8	13 + 1	12 + 2	4 + 8	3 + 9	6 + 8	11 + 2	8 + 5	5 + 8	6 + 7	10 + 3
4 + 7	7 + 6	6 + 7	11 + 3	0 + 14	1 + 13	6 + 6	7 + 5	7 + 7	12 + 1	1 + 12	13 + 0	0 + 13	7 + 6
5 + 6	5 + 8	8 + 5	1 + 14	0 + 15	8 + 7	7 + 8	15 + 0	8 + 7	14 + 1	7 + 8	0 + 15	8 + 7	3 + 10
8 + 3	4 + 9	9 + 4	2 + 13	3 + 12	4 + 11	5 + 10	6 + 9	7 + 8	9 + 6	8 + 7	10 + 5	1 + 14	2 + 11
4 + 7	3 + 10	10 + 3	3 + 12	2 + 13	1 + 14	0 + 15	9 + 5	5 + 9	7 + 7	6 + 8	8 + 6	2 + 13	11 + 2
3 + 8	1 + 12	2 + 11	7 + 8	5 + 10	4 + 11	12 + 3	11 + 4	7 + 8	4 + 10	8 + 7	10 + 4	3 + 12	6 + 7
7 + 4	11 + 2	3 + 10	15 + 0	7 + 8	6 + 9	13 + 2	10 + 5	9 + 6	8 + 7	7 + 8	6 + 9	4 + 11	10 + 3
9 + 2	4 + 9	10 + 3	11 + 4	14 + 1	13 + 2	8 + 7	15 + 0	14 + 1	13 + 2	12 + 3	11 + 4	5 + 10	7 + 6
8 + 3	8 + 5	9 + 4	12 + 3	12 + 3	2 + 13	12 + 3	11 + 4	10 + 5	7 + 8	9 + 6	8 + 7	7 + 8	3 + 10
2 + 9	2 + 11	5 + 8	8 + 7	9 + 6	10 + 5	6 + 9	7 + 7	5 + 9	6 + 8	9 + 5	8 + 6	0 + 15	9 + 4
3 + 8	6 + 7	7 + 6	6 + 9	0 + 15	8 + 7	11 + 4	15 + 0	12 + 3	10 + 5	7 + 8	2 + 13	1 + 14	8 + 5
1 + 10	9 + 4	5 + 8	15 + 0	14 + 1	6 + 9	4 + 11	12 + 3	13 + 2	7 + 8	9 + 6	6 + 9	3 + 12	6 + 7
9 + 2	3 + 10	4 + 9	9 + 6	1 + 14	9 + 6	5 + 10	9 + 6	14 + 1	11 + 4	8 + 7	5 + 10	4 + 11	4 + 9
10 + 1	8 + 5	0 + 13	13 + 2	2 + 13	8 + 7	6 + 9	7 + 7	6 + 9	4 + 10	11 + 3	10 + 4	2 + 13	5 + 8
2 + 9	13 + 0	12 + 1	3 + 12	7 + 8	6 + 9	8 + 7	13 + 1	2 + 12	2 + 12	1 + 14	3 + 11	3 + 12	7 + 6
11 + 0	10 + 3	1 + 12	12 + 3	11 + 4	12 + 3	7 + 8	6 + 9	8 + 7	5 + 10	4 + 11	0 + 15	15 + 0	3 + 10
8 + 3	12 + 1	11 + 2	4 + 11	10 + 5	13 + 2	14 + 1	15 + 0	14 + 1	12 + 3	7 + 8	9 + 6	14 + 1	8 + 5
0 + 11	6 + 4	2 + 8	3 + 7	2 + 13	7 + 8	6 + 9	5 + 10	2 + 13	13 + 2	11 + 4	10 + 5	8 + 7	4 + 9
3 + 8	1 + 9	6 + 6	8 + 2	13 + 2	15 + 0	9 + 6	7 + 7	8 + 6	6 + 8	0 + 14	1 + 13	15 + 0	5 + 8
5 + 6	7 + 3	5 + 5	4 + 6	12 + 3	14 + 1	8 + 7	2 + 13	13 + 2	14 + 0	8 + 7	14 + 1	13 + 2	7 + 6
7 + 4	7 + 6	6 + 7	8 + 7	3 + 12	13 + 2	7 + 8	6 + 8	9 + 5	5 + 9	3 + 11	8 + 6	12 + 3	9 + 4
6 + 5	2 + 11	4 + 9	9 + 6	4 + 11	5 + 10	6 + 9	7 + 8	8 + 7	9 + 6	10 + 5	11 + 4	7 + 8	6 + 7
4 + 7	5 + 8	12 + 1	13 + 0	6 + 7	0 + 13	7 + 6	9 + 4	1 + 12	2 + 11	4 + 9	3 + 10	5 + 8	4 + 9

To complete this mosaic, color the facts using the key.

yellow 13   red 14   light blue 15   dark blue 16   green 17   orange 18

8 + 8	4 + 12	3 + 13	2 + 14	1 + 15	0 + 16	16 + 0	3 + 15	15 + 1	14 + 2	13 + 3	12 + 4	11 + 5	10 + 6	9 + 7	8 + 8	
14 + 2	16 + 0	11 + 5	3 + 13	10 + 6	1 + 17	2 + 16	13 + 5	12 + 6	11 + 7	16 + 0	11 + 5	10 + 6	11 + 2	6 + 10	7 + 9	
13 + 3	12 + 4	6 + 10	13 + 3	2 + 14	1 + 15	6 + 7	10 + 3	9 + 4	15 + 1	12 + 4	9 + 7	12 + 1	5 + 8	8 + 5	5 + 11	
12 + 4	9 + 7	7 + 9	4 + 12	0 + 16	3 + 13	4 + 9	7 + 6	3 + 10	14 + 2	8 + 8	1 + 12	4 + 9	10 + 3	3 + 10	7 + 6	
11 + 5	15 + 1	10 + 6	14 + 2	1 + 15	2 + 14	5 + 8	2 + 11	8 + 5	13 + 3	7 + 9	6 + 10	0 + 13	9 + 4	6 + 7	4 + 12	
9 + 7	8 + 8	9 + 7	5 + 11	0 + 16	4 + 14	7 + 11	8 + 10	9 + 9	10 + 8	5 + 11	15 + 1	14 + 2	13 + 0	0 + 16	3 + 13	
14 + 2	7 + 9	5 + 11	10 + 6	9 + 7	5 + 13	15 + 3	9 + 4	12 + 6	11 + 7	4 + 12	16 + 0	13 + 3	12 + 4	1 + 15	2 + 14	
9 + 7	6 + 10	8 + 8	6 + 10	13 + 3	6 + 12	16 + 2	4 + 14	13 + 5	14 + 4	3 + 13	4 + 12	11 + 5	11 + 5	2 + 14	1 + 15	
15 + 1	7 + 9	11 + 5	12 + 4	8 + 8	17 + 1	15 + 3	4 + 9	7 + 11	8 + 10	2 + 14	3 + 13	8 + 8	10 + 6	3 + 13	0 + 16	
10 + 6	5 + 11	7 + 9	10 + 6	11 + 5	18 + 0	14 + 4	11 + 7	16 + 2	10 + 8	1 + 15	2 + 14	9 + 7	5 + 11	4 + 12	5 + 11	
8 + 8	6 + 10	8 + 8	4 + 12	9 + 7	5 + 13	5 + 8	2 + 16	3 + 10	9 + 9	0 + 16	1 + 15	4 + 12	7 + 9	8 + 8	6 + 10	
7 + 9	5 + 11	7 + 9	12 + 4	13 + 3	13 + 5	12 + 6	8 + 10	3 + 15	8 + 10	5 + 11	0 + 16	3 + 13	6 + 10	0 + 16	9 + 7	
6 + 10	4 + 12	9 + 7	6 + 10	9 + 7	6 + 12	8 + 5	9 + 9	10 + 3	7 + 11	6 + 10	4 + 12	7 + 9	1 + 15	10 + 6	11 + 5	
5 + 11	3 + 13	15 + 1	14 + 2	8 + 8	7 + 11	17 + 1	10 + 8	9 + 9	14 + 4	9 + 7	12 + 4	2 + 14	15 + 1	14 + 2	12 + 4	
16 + 0	2 + 14	7 + 9	5 + 11	7 + 9	8 + 10	7 + 6	8 + 10	11 + 2	8 + 10	8 + 8	3 + 13	13 + 3	1 + 15	13 + 3	14 + 2	
8 + 8	1 + 15	2 + 14	3 + 13	4 + 12	1 + 17	6 + 12	14 + 4	9 + 9	11 + 7	4 + 12	10 + 6	9 + 7	16 + 0	2 + 14	16 + 0	
9 + 7	0 + 16	7 + 9	1 + 15	0 + 16	9 + 9	6 + 7	13 + 5	2 + 11	10 + 8	5 + 11	14 + 2	13 + 3	11 + 5	9 + 7	6 + 10	
7 + 9	16 + 0	8 + 8	9 + 7	8 + 8	10 + 8	15 + 3	0 + 18	11 + 7	12 + 6	16 + 0	15 + 1	12 + 4	10 + 6	8 + 8	7 + 9	
8 + 7	5 + 10	2 + 13	6 + 9	10 + 5	16 + 2	12 + 6	8 + 6	10 + 8	13 + 5	2 + 13	15 + 0	14 + 1	8 + 7	0 + 15	13 + 2	
4 + 11	7 + 8	1 + 14	14 + 1	0 + 15	18 + 0	17 + 1	7 + 7	7 + 11	18 + 0	1 + 14	7 + 8	9 + 6	5 + 10	4 + 11	14 + 1	
11 + 4	13 + 2	9 + 6	15 + 0	8 + 9	12 + 5	7 + 10	10 + 7	9 + 8	15 + 2	2 + 15	8 + 9	6 + 9	10 + 5	11 + 4	1 + 14	
3 + 12	12 + 3	6 + 11	7 + 10	5 + 12	4 + 13	8 + 9	11 + 6	8 + 9	10 + 7	9 + 8	1 + 16	16 + 1	0 + 17	12 + 3	0 + 15	
7 + 8	9 + 8	10 + 7	11 + 6	13 + 4	3 + 14	9 + 8	14 + 3	6 + 11	5 + 12	4 + 13	3 + 14	2 + 15	1 + 16	17 + 0	15 + 0	
8 + 7	10 + 5	4 + 11	3 + 12	13 + 2	9 + 6	5 + 10	2 + 13	9 + 6	7 + 8	6 + 9	1 + 14	2 + 13	14 + 1	8 + 7	14 + 1	
9 + 6	5 + 10	11 + 4	12 + 3	8 + 7	11 + 4	10 + 5	6 + 9	8 + 7	13 + 2	4 + 11	3 + 12	12 + 3	13 + 2	15 + 0	7 + 8	

Draw lines from one answer to the next after working out the algorithms. Start at number one.

1. 20 + 40 + 20 = ☐
2. 60 + 70 + 60 = ☐
3. 20 + 30 + 50 = ☐
4. 30 + 30 + 30 = ☐
5. 10 + 10 + 10 = ☐
6. 70 + 40 + 90 = ☐
7. 80 + 80 + 70 = ☐
8. 100 + 90 + 90 = ☐
9. 120 + 50 + 130 = ☐
10. 30 + 20 + 10 = ☐
11. 90 + 90 + 110 = ☐
12. 80 + 60 + 70 = ☐
13. 30 + 20 + 60 = ☐
14. 30 + 40 + 70 = ☐

15. 80 + 70 + 70 = ☐
16. 10 + 20 + 10 = ☐
17. 80 + 80 + 80 = ☐
18. 20 + 30 + 20 = ☐
19. 40 + 40 + 40 = ☐
20. 40 + 70 + 40 = ☐
21. 50 + 70 + 50 = ☐
22. 20 + 10 + 20 = ☐
23. 80 + 90 + 80 = ☐
24. 30 + 90 + 60 = ☐
25. 20 + 50 + 60 = ☐
26. 90 + 80 + 90 = ☐
27. 40 + 80 + 40 = ☐
28. 90 + 90 + 90 = ☐

29. 130 + 90 + 90 = ☐
30. 30 + 20 + 30 = ☐

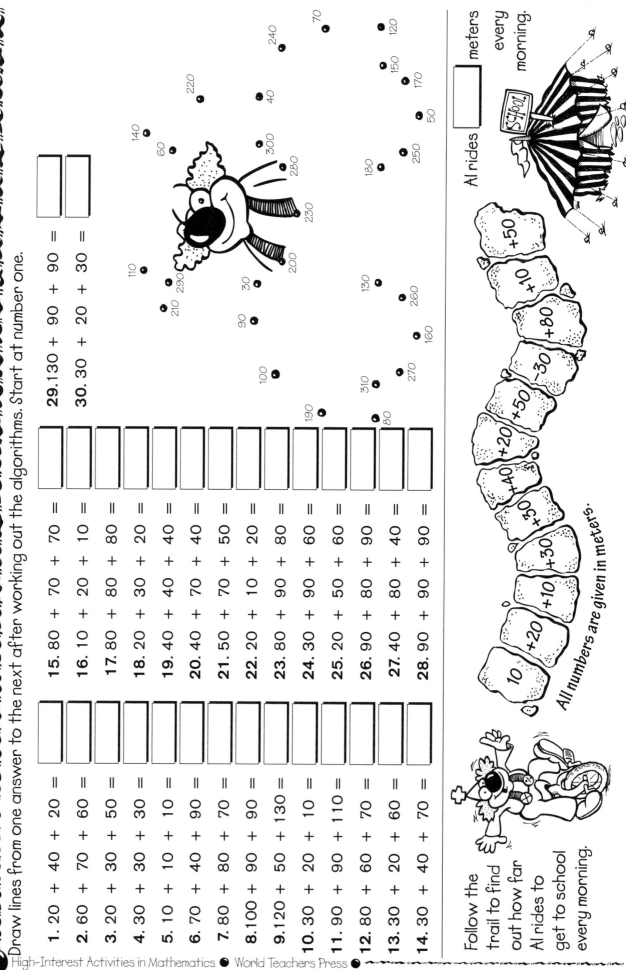

Follow the trail to find out how far Al rides to get to school every morning.

All numbers are given in meters.

10 +20 +10 +30 +30 +40 +20 +50 -30 +80 +10 +50

Al rides ☐ meters every morning.

Vowel and Consonant Addition

Jim is having a sale. Each grocery item costs 5¢ for each vowel and 10¢ for each consonant. How much would the sale items below cost?

1. soap = 10¢ + 5¢ + 5¢ + 10¢ = 30¢

2. milk = _____ = _____

3. salt = _____ = _____

4. pepper = _____ = _____

5. margarine = _____ = _____

6. bread = _____ = _____

7. carrots = _____ = _____

8. celery = _____ = _____

9. cabbage = _____ = _____

10. onions = _____ = _____

11. pickles = _____ = _____

12. garlic = _____ = _____

13. ginger = _____ = _____

14. jelly = _____ = _____

15. melons = _____ = _____

16. flour = _____ = _____

17. chicken = _____ = _____

18. cheese = _____ = _____

19. licorice = _____ = _____

20. plums = _____ = _____

21. lemons = _____ = _____

22. honey = _____ = _____

23. birdseed = _____ = _____

24. popcorn = _____ = _____

25. fish = _____ = _____

By matching the coded letter with its number in the answers, you will find the names of the ships that made up the First Fleet, which sailed from England to Australia in 1788, beginning the European settlement of the South Pacific.

Code:
A = 35, B = 27, C = 18, D = 19, E = 40, F = 28, G = 20, H = 38, I = 37, J = 26, K = 29, L = 25, M = 24, N = 16, O = 21, P = 36, Q = 23, R = 39, S = 41, T = 22, U = 17, V = 30, W = 34, X = 33, Y = 32, Z = 31

Problem 1

8	9	9	5	3	9
8	8	8	9	5	9
9	7	4	7	3	5
8	9	9	8	3	9
+8	+4	+9	+8	+3	+9

Problem 2

8	4	8	6	4	6
9	2	7	9	4	6
7	3	7	5	9	8
8	4	7	9	4	6
+9	+4	+7	+7	+4	+6

Problem 3

7	8	8	7	7	3	3	9	8
7	3	5	8	6	4	5	4	8
7	3	9	7	8	3	2	9	7
7	8	9	5	5	3	4	9	8
+7	+3	+9	+6	+9	+3	+5	+9	+8

Problem 4

3	7	9	5	6	5	4	5	9
4	9	4	9	7	6	6	4	7
3	8	8	9	5	3	4	4	6
6	6	7	9	3	4	4	4	9
+2	+8	+7	+7	+4	+3	+4	+5	+9

Problem 5

5	7	9	8	2	4	9	9	9	6
8	9	5	8	4	4	9	9	8	9
6	8	7	7	2	3	7	7	2	9
4	7	9	9	5	4	7	8	9	5
+5	+8	+7	+8	+3	+4	+9	+4	+9	+7

Problem 6

8	8	6	8	9	7	2
7	9	3	9	3	5	3
6	7	1	8	8	7	6
7	9	2	9	9	9	2
+8	+7	+4	+4	+9	+7	+3

Lady

Problem 7

9	6	9	2	3	8
8	9	7	4	4	7
7	7	7	1	5	9
6	9	7	7	2	7
+6	+8	+7	+2	+4	+9

Problem 8

6	6
5	8
4	5
2	6
+4	+3

Problem 9

9	8	5	8	9
6	8	5	9	8
4	6	5	8	8
8	9	5	8	8
+7	+4	+5	+8	+8

Problem 10

9	3	5	9	8	4	9	5	2	4	9
9	3	7	7	5	3	8	3	4	4	8
7	4	9	8	6	7	7	6	5	4	7
9	4	6	9	4	5	8	2	2	4	8
+7	+4	+8	+6	+4	+2	+7	+5	+4	+4	+6

Problem 11

9	7	5	6	6	6	5	6	6	5	9
8	6	9	8	7	7	3	9	5	5	9
2	2	3	8	2	8	4	4	9	4	9
3	3	9	9	2	5	5	4	3	9	9
+5	+3	+7	+8	+4	+8	+2	+7	+7	+8	

Problem 12

6	8	9	7	5	1	7	3
4	7	8	8	5	5	8	2
3	7	7	8	7	1	7	3
8	8	9	8	6	1	8	3
+7	+7	+8	+7	+4	+5	+9	+5

Problem 13

6	5	8	5	9	2
4	5	6	2	7	7
2	5	7	2	9	2
3	1	1	4	6	3
+5	+5	+3	+6	+9	+2

Problem 14

7	9	4	6	8
4	6	5	6	8
3	6	4	6	9
3	9	4	6	9
+3	+9	+4	+6	+6

Addition Code II

By matching the coded letter with its number in the answers, you will find the words to fill the blanks in the story.

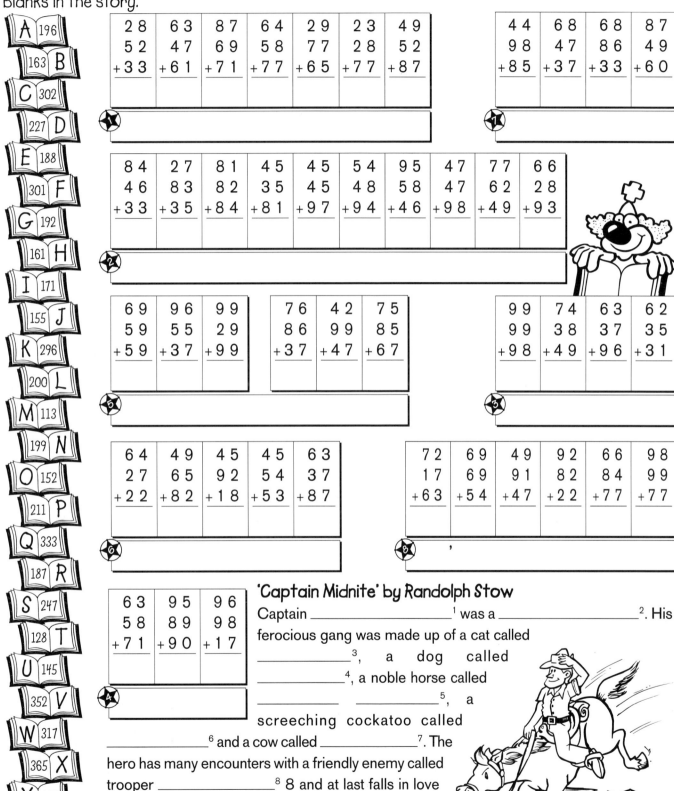

Code key:

A 196	B 163	C 302	D 227	E 188	F 301	G 192	H 161	I 171	J 155	K 296	L 200	M 113
N 199	O 152	P 211	Q 333	R 187	S 247	T 128	U 145	V 352	W 317	X 365	Y 274	Z 311

1.

28	63	87	64	29	23	49
52	47	69	58	77	28	52
+33	+61	+71	+77	+65	+77	+87

7.

44	68	68	87
98	47	86	49
+85	+37	+33	+60

2.

84	27	81	45	45	54	95	47	77	66
46	83	82	35	45	48	58	47	62	28
+33	+35	+84	+81	+97	+94	+46	+98	+49	+93

5.

69	96	99
59	55	29
+59	+37	+99

76	42	75
86	99	85
+37	+47	+67

3.

99	74	63	62
99	38	37	35
+98	+49	+96	+31

6.

64	49	45	45	63
27	65	92	54	37
+22	+82	+18	+53	+87

8.

72	69	49	92	66	98
17	69	91	82	84	99
+63	+54	+47	+22	+77	+77

4.

63	95	96
58	89	98
+71	+90	+17

'Captain Midnite' by Randolph Stow

Captain _____[1] was a _____[2]. His ferocious gang was made up of a cat called _____[3], a dog called _____[4], a noble horse called _____ _____[5], a screeching cockatoo called _____[6] and a cow called _____[7]. The hero has many encounters with a friendly enemy called trooper _____[8] 8 and at last falls in love with the great beauty of the day, the incredibly attractive Miss Laura Wellborn.

Addition Code III

Solve the problem below and then use the code to find the letters in each word. Use the words to complete the story.

$ 7.66	$ 8.77	$ 5.92	$ 6.68	$ 6.65	$ 5.37	$ 5.87
7.69	7.88	5.63	8.53	8.42	5.61	4.21
+ 7.77	+ 7.79	+ 7.48	+ 4.67	+ 7.15	+ 3.98	+ 7.21

❸ _____

$ 6.44	$ 9.08	$ 5.77	$ 8.06	$ 6.84	$ 9.42	$ 4.91
8.62	6.77	5.39	5.75	5.54	9.54	6.39
+ 7.15	+ 7.26	+ 8.72	+ 9.30	+ 3.17	+ 5.48	+ 5.58

❹ _____

$ 9.99	$ 6.88	$ 4.23	$ 4.16	$ 8.88	$ 8.88	$ 8.49
9.81	5.27	5.11	4.48	9.77	7.78	8.45
+ 6.87	+ 5.14	+ 5.62	+ 6.32	+ 4.63	+ 7.78	+ 8.27

❺ _____

$ 5.65	$ 8.03	$ 8.48	$ 7.36	$ 8.49	$ 9.63
8.47	8.08	7.24	7.74	9.58	5.49
+ 5.76	+ 8.04	+ 8.72	+ 7.35	+ 4.38	+ 9.32

❶ _____

$ 5.47	$ 6.35	$ 4.44	$ 7.77	$ 6.32	$ 5.92
3.51	9.48	5.55	6.58	4.28	6.45
+ 5.98	+ 6.62	+ 4.97	+ 8.77	+ 4.36	+ 4.51

❷ _____

We are lucky to be living in exciting times. In 1969 the members of the _____[1] _____[2] mission walked on the moon. Now we are looking further out into the heavens. The _____[3] space probe has already sent back more information about our Solar System than we gathered in all the years before. In 1989, President George Bush announced the plan to build a _____[4] in space called _____[5] with the ultimate intention of sending people to land on Mars.

Comets and meteors travel at about 80 km/s, 40 times the speed of a bullet!

Code:

A	$19.88	B	$23.45
C	$20.02	D	$23.28
E	$14.96	F	$26.67
G	$22.22	H	$24.27
I	$15.55	J	$23.15
K	$20.03	L	$22.45
M	$25.21	N	$16.88
O	$24.44	P	$24.15
Q	$25.16	R	$17.29
S	$22.21	T	$23.11
U	$18.81	V	$23.12
W	$20.12	X	$23.69
Y	$19.03	Z	$21.11

By matching the coded letter with its number in the answers you will make the words to fill the blanks in the story below.

612 −395	660 −429	488 −365	645 −417	452 −289

☐ ☐ ☐ ☐ ☐

715 −498	423 −229	491 −368	635 −388	533 −318	616 −359

☐ ☐ ☐ ☐ ☐ ☐

532 −409	350 −117	401 −168	564 −441

☐ ☐ ☐ ☐

406 −267	779 −585	400 −252	330 −136	800 −569	705 −474

☐ ☐ ☐ ☐ ☐ ☐

600 −423	723 −527	513 −319	666 −489

☐ ☐ ☐ ☐

611 −472	814 −557	420 −229	928 −675	670 −547	613 −398	516 −389	700 −443

☐ ☐ ☐ ☐ ☐ ☐ ☐ ☐

500 −361	700 −453	666 −444	420 −198	442 −248	463 −217	484 −288	804 −571	614 −365

☐ ☐ ☐ ☐ ☐ ☐ ☐ ☐ ☐

A 123   B 211   C 228   D 177   E 194   F 222   G 249   H 127   I 196   J 185   K 163   L 231   M 191

N 233   O 135   P 253   Q 204   R 246   S 139   T 215   U 241   V 235   W 148   X 209   Y 251   Z 152

"_____ _____" is the only book

_____ _____ ever wrote. It was

published just a few months before she _____ . She

was never to know of its great success. It tells the story of a

horse's life with great _____ . The author's

aim was to make people aware of the

_____ horses endured.

Match the coded letter with the amounts in the answers, to make the words to fill the blanks below.
Put the words in the correct order so the story makes sense.

$12.67	$13.91	$15.23	$12.95	$15.36	$13.85	$10.01	$16.43	$10.25	$12.22	$14.89	$10.28	$16.59
A	B	C	D	E	F	G	H	I	J	K	L	M

$10.35	$14.65	$15.86	$10.37	$14.77	$15.55	$13.99	$12.18	$11.56	$10.38	$11.39	$10.45	$10.57
N	O	P	Q	R	S	T	U	V	W	X	Y	Z

1

$93.20 − 79.35

$72.32 − 57.67

$81.41 − 66.76

$78.23 − 65.28

JAM

2

$48.48 − 31.89

$47.29 − 32.64

$48.50 − 31.91

3

$58.03 − 45.08

$44.71 − 32.04

$67.12 − 54.17

JAM

4

$94.21 − 80.36

$32.69 − 20.02

$61.74 − 47.75

JAM

5

$32.91 − 22.90

$66.38 − 53.71

$51.17 − 35.62

JAM JAM JAM

6

$67.89 − 53.98

$62.22 − 47.57

$49.98 − 37.03

$47.32 − 37.07

$29.21 − 13.85

$24.33 − 8.78

7

$62.03 − 46.67

$31.58 − 18.91

$52.17 − 38.18

JAM

8

$53.37 − 37.82

$53.79 − 41.12

$69.57 − 59.29

$70.31 − 56.32

9

$49.33 − 33.78

$48.01 − 35.83

$27.49 − 17.48

$57.83 − 45.16

$82.45 − 67.68

$84.21 − 68.98

$36.63 − 23.96

$86.49 − 71.72

10

'You are what you _____ [1] ' is a popular saying. I'm sure _____ [2] or _____ [3] wouldn't put the wrong

_____ [4] in the family _____ [5] . Yet we fill our _____ [6] with the wrong kind of _____ [7].

Watch carefully the amounts of _____ [8] , _____ [9] and _____ [10] you eat.

Multiplication Code I

By matching the coded letter with its number in the answers, you will make the words to fill the blanks below.

A 1440 · B 5280 · C 3960 · D 1080 · E 960 · F 2000 · G 2040 · H 2520 · I 1560 · J 480 · K 880 · L 3360 · M 2760
N 840 · O 1680 · P 3720 · Q 4030 · R 2880 · S 3240 · T 2640 · U 3480 · V 490 · W 360 · X 550 · Y 770 · Z 990

16 x 30	96 x 30	32 x 90	88 x 30	84 x 20	84 x 40	44 x 20	52 x 30	32 x 30	42 x 20

44 x 60	84 x 30	16 x 60	42 x 60	56 x 30	132 x 40	264 x 20	39 x 40	88 x 30

48 x 30	36 x 30	7 x 70	48 x 20	21 x 40	66 x 40	87 x 40	48 x 60	24 x 40

176 x 30	26 x 60	168 x 20	88 x 60	21 x 80

66 x 80	24 x 60	68 x 30	34 x 60	78 x 20	28 x 30	81 x 40

_____ wrote the story, "_____" for his children. The story tells of a great _____ had by the main character, _____ . Together with some dwarfs he goes seeking a long lost treasure and encounters many terrors on the way.

High-Interest Activities in Mathematics ● World Teachers Press ● Page 15

By matching the coded letter with its number in the answers, you will find the names of some characters to fill the blanks below.

A 2904 B 757 C 493 D 1196 E 1728
F 1925 G 817 H 666 I 1781 J 1492
K 1888 L 2079 M 1248 N 1961
O 736 P 2234 Q 1849
R 768 S 2178 T 1088
U 1915 V 1066
W 1855 X 1770
Y 1986 Z 1930

24 x 32	66 x 44	34 x 32

52 x 24	32 x 23	63 x 33	48 x 36

64 x 17	46 x 16	88 x 33	52 x 23

53 x 35	96 x 18	132 x 22	99 x 22	72 x 24	99 x 21	66 x 33

55 x 35	54 x 32	64 x 12	48 x 16	64 x 27	34 x 32	121 x 18

'Wind in the Willows', written by Kenneth Grahame, tells of the adventures of a _____ , _____

and _____ in the English countryside. With their friend, Badger, they have a great battle with some

_____ , _____ and stoats to win back the mansion, Toad Hall.

You can make up a story for just about any math algorithm.

For example: For 7 – 3 = 4 (seven take away three) you could write this little story:

'There were seven apples in a tree. Three fell off, leaving four.'

Make up a little math story about these number sentences:

1. 6 + 3 _____

_____

2. 8 – 5 _____

_____

3. 6 x 2 _____

_____

4. 9 ÷ 4 _____

_____

Remember: Division can be thought of as sharing.

Draw a cartoon strip to illustrate one of your math stories.

Algorithm: _____

Story: _____

_____

Drawing:

Dream Home

The picture below shows a plan of a house drawn from a top view.

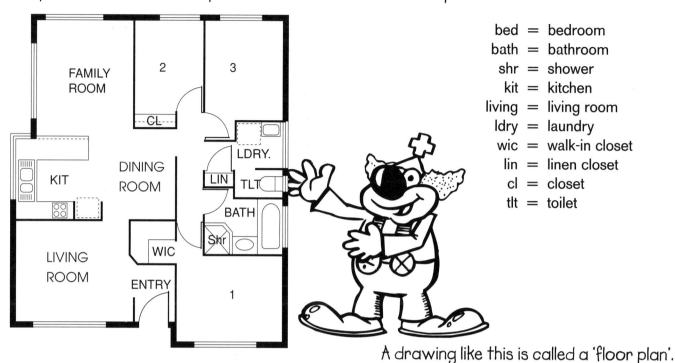

bed = bedroom
bath = bathroom
shr = shower
kit = kitchen
living = living room
ldry = laundry
wic = walk-in closet
lin = linen closet
cl = closet
tlt = toilet

A drawing like this is called a 'floor plan'.

Draw a top view of your own "dream home".

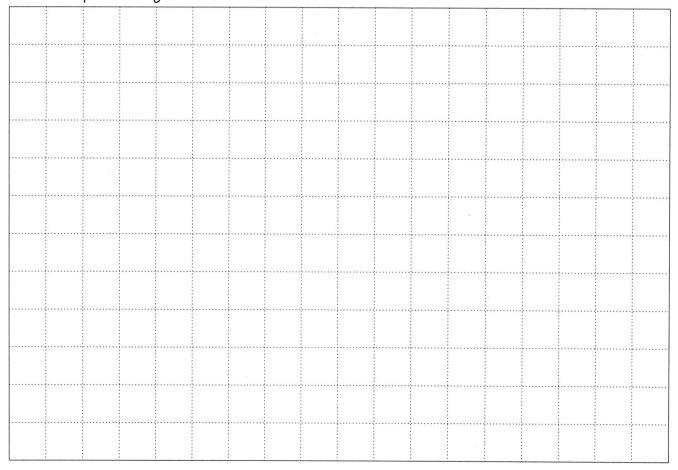

Fill in the blanks. Follow the rule to get your answer.

1. Rule: □ = △² + (3 × ○)

□									
△	3	6	7	12	8	12	4	8	10
○	9	2	3	4	12	9	12	4	6

2. Rule: ☼ = (☺ × 4) − 🦁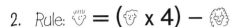

☼									38					
☺	3	6	5	12	10	1	7	0	11	8	2	9	4	5
🦁	6	10	9	25	39	3	0	0		6	7	11	5	15

3. Rule: ☮ = (🎈 + 5) − 🌻

☮														
🎈	7	10	20	9	14	15	12	100	17	13	11	16	8	5
🌻	6	13	24	11	19	1	17	55	20	8	7	13	12	5

4. Rule: ◉ = (○ × 3) ÷ ●

◉														
○	3	6	7	12	8	12	4	8	10	0	8	10	8	12
●	9	2	3	4	12	9	12	4	6	6	6	5	2	6

5. Rule: ▯ = (▲ − 4) + (◖ × 2)

▮														9
▲	8	9	7	10	6	7	5	11	4	12	5	8	6	7
◖	3	11	8	7	12	6	9	10	0	1	5	2	4	

6. Rule: ⊠ = (▮ × 2) − ▤

⊠							0							
▮	3	6	8	5	10	2	12	7	5	1	11	9	4	12
▤	6	5	11	9	17	4	21		1	1	20	3	1	12

Fill in the blanks. Follow the rule to get your answer.

1. Rule: $X^2 + 1 = Y$

X	3	5	10	12	2	1	$\frac{1}{2}$		30		
Y								17		37	82

2. Rule: $A^2 + B^2 = C$

A	2	7	3	1	3	5	7	9	2	1	3	6	2	5	
B	3	4	6	7		8	6	8	11						7
C					14					1	34	136	85	$25\frac{1}{4}$	74

3. Rule: $2N + 3Q = D$ Expands to: $(2 \times N) + (3 \times Q) = D$

N	3	6	2	1	4	2	5	6	2	3			5	7	
Q	5	4	9	3	6	7	8	7	10	4	8	5			11
D	21										30	25	34	44	43

4. Rule: $3B - P = \frac{1}{2}F$ Expands to: $(3 \times B) - P = (\frac{1}{2} \times F)$

B	9	8	2	7	8	5	7	2	12	7	6		11	1	5
P	2	6	5	6	2	10	4	4	18	14		8		3	
F											24	44	10		30

5. Rule: $\frac{1}{2}X + Y = Z$

X	6	8	4	12	22	14	8	10	30	2	5	3	17		$\frac{1}{4}$
Y	7	5	9	2	1	4	3	6	8		6	3		1	8
Z										8			$9\frac{1}{2}$	$2\frac{1}{2}$	

6. Rule: $B^2 + \frac{1}{2}C = D$

B	6	9	3	8	4	7	5	10	12	1	4	11		5	
C	4	10	16	22	28	8	14	12	16	50	3	15	8	7	$\frac{1}{2}$
D													29		$16\frac{1}{4}$

7. Rule: $(3P + 5) - Q = R$

P	7	9	8	6	5	3	6	10	12	11	13	1	0	7	
Q	26	19	9	12	7	14	9	5	6			7	$\frac{1}{2}$	$5\frac{1}{2}$	$1\frac{1}{2}$
R										37	30				$27\frac{1}{2}$

Graphing and Probability

Probability means the likelihood of something happening. When we toss a coin there are two probable outcomes. They are that the coin will show heads or show tails.

Alison and Rebecca tested the probability of a coin landing heads or tails. They wrote the result of each throw and tallied it before making a column graph to show the results. 'H' stands for heads and 'T' stands for tails.

Throw No.	1	2	3	4	5	6	7	8	9	10	11	12	13	14	15	16	17	18	19	20
Result	H	T	H	T	T	T	H	T	H	T	T	H	H	T	H	T	T	H	T	H

Tally

Heads	ЖЖ IIII
Tails	ЖЖ ЖЖ I

Column Graph

Heads											
Tails											

Activity One

With a partner, toss a coin 20 times. Tally the results and show them on the column graph.

Throw No.	1	2	3	4	5	6	7	8	9	10	11	12	13	14	15	16	17	18	19	20
Result																				

Tally

Heads	
Tails	

Column Graph

Heads											
Tails											

Activity Two

When two coins are tossed there are three possible outcomes. They are that the coins will show two heads (H-H), two tails (T-T) or one head and one tail (H-T). With a partner, toss two coins together 20 times. Tally the results and show them on the column graph.

Throw No.	1	2	3	4	5	6	7	8	9	10	11	12	13	14	15	16	17	18	19	20
Result																				

Tally

H – H	
H – T	
T – T	

Column Graph

H – H													
H – T													
T – T													

QUIZ Which result came up more often? Why do you think this happened?

Calculator Story

You can use your calculator to write stories as well as do long, difficult mathematical calculations. Use your calculator to do the following calculation: $5318 \times 1000 + 804$. Your answer should be 5318804. Turn your calculator upside down. Can you see that this answer spells the word "hobbies"? Do the calculations in the story below, turn your calculator upside down and write the words in the blank spaces.

1. $40 \times 10 + 38 + 76$
2. $33 \times 33 \times 33 - 931$
3. $1\,000\,000 \div 200 + 2735$
4. $36 \times 10 + 154$
5. $2\,000 \times 10 + 15\,000 + 336$
6. $500\,000 \div 10 \div 5 - 5\,000 + 663$
7. $20 \times 20 \times 20 - 895$
8. $304 \times 5 \times 2 + 5$
9. $53 \times 3 \times 3 + 24 \times 10 + 328$
10. $65 \times 12 - 173$
11. $5\,000 \div 10 \div 5 - 68 + 2$
12. $44 \times 100 + 1\,300 - 63$
13. $25 \times 2 \times 2 \times 2 + 30 \times 9 - 3\,285$
14. $451 \times 100 \times 100 + 7\,734$
15. $23 \times 20 \times 5 \times 2 + 70 - 56$
16. $54 \times 200 \times 50 - 2\,000 + 76$
17. $45 \times 3 \times 3 \times 10 + 456$
18. $28 \times 2\,000 + 2\,000 - 262$
19. $45 \times 3 \times 2 + 39 \times 2$
20. $77 + 7\,000 + 700 - 59$
21. $33 \times 33 \times 2 + 3\,003$
22. $352\,500 + 28\,052 - 1746$
23. $13 \times 100 + 34$
24. $40 \times 20 \times 9 \times 7 \times 3 \times 3 + 130\,000 - 6\,255$
25. $65 \div 5 \times 3\,000 - 3\,993$
26. $45 \times 2 - 19 \times 100 + 5$
27. $35 + 7\,000 + 456 + 244$
28. $5\,773 \times 100 + 45$
29. $23 + 10 \times 33 \times 3 + 109$
30. $450 \times 1\,000 + 45$
31. $3\,788 \times 100 + 4$
32. $123 \times 45 - 12 + 210$

One day a farmer was driving _____[1] _____[2] to market to _____[3]. It was the eldest of _____[4] _____[5] and could no longer give _____[6]. He stopped to remove some _____[7] from his _____[8]. Suddenly some _____[9] came flying from a _____[10]. "Shoo!" _____[11] shouted. He was stung on the hands and _____[12]. They passed by the wheat _____[13]. All of a sudden there was a _____[14] noise. _____[15] up in the sky he saw some shiny _____[16]. "_____![17]" he said to himself. They made a noise like the clanging of thousands of _____[18]. One of the mysterious objects landed and out stepped a _____[19] bird with a _____[20] like a duck and a body like an _____[21]. It began to _____[22] like a turkey. The goose understood what it said. To the farmer's surprise his goose began to speak to him. "Look under you left _____[23] and you will find some magic _____[24] in the _____[25] _____[26]. Do not _____[27] your goose. The old man of the forest will be there. He will tell you what you must do."

The farmer dug in the soft ground and found the _____[28].

Filled with _____[29] he ran to the market. He saw the old man of the forest and began to tell him what had happened.

"_____![30] You must speak quietly," said the old man.

"Throw the shells into the pond," he said. "Now I must _____[31] off. Do everything just as I have told you."

The farmer did as he was told. The water began to churn and bubble. Two large _____[32] slid up onto the bank of the pond. In their mouths each had a beautiful jewel. They dropped their jewels and vanished in the murky waters. The farmer never had to worry about money again. He certainly did not sell his wonderful goose.

Magic squares are thousands of years old. No one knows where they originated, but they were known to exist in China earlier than 1000 BC.

Vertical rows, horizontal rows and diagonals all add up to the same amount in magic squares. This total is known as the "magic number" or "constant". Write the magic number in the star as shown in the example.

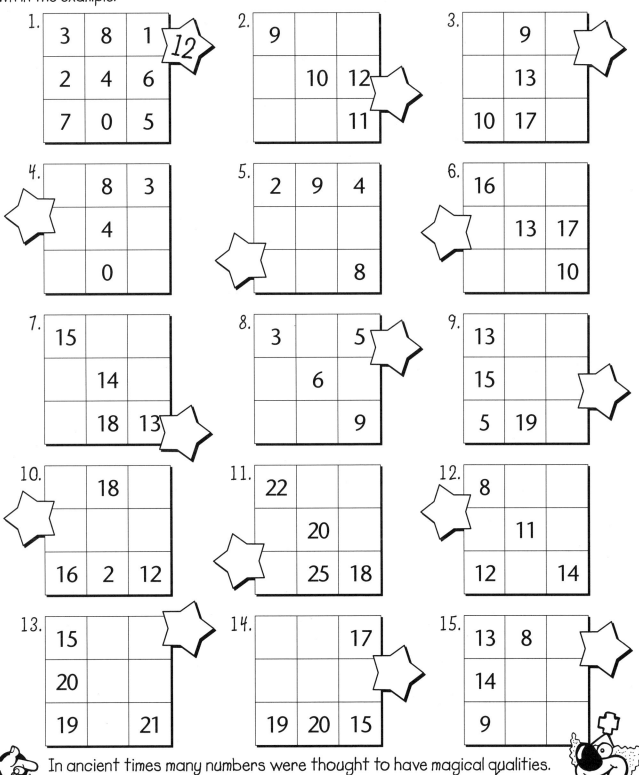

In ancient times many numbers were thought to have magical qualities. Similarly, magic squares were thought to possess special qualities.

4	5	16	9
14	11	2	7
1	8	13	12
15	10	3	6

This magic square is called a "diabolical".

The horizontal, vertical and diagonal rows all add up to 34. There are, however, many more combinations of four numbers in the square that total 34. In all, there are 86 such combinations. Put the missing number from the magic square in each group to make it total 34. Remember to use only the numbers 1 to 16.

1. 1, 2, 15, ___
2. 1, 3, 14, ___
3. 1, 3, 13, ___
4. 1, 4, 14, ___
5. 1, 5, 12, ___
6. 1, 5, 13, ___
7. 1, 6, 11, ___
8. 1, 6, 12, ___
9. 1, 6, 13, ___
10. 1, 7, 10, ___
11. 1, 7, 11, ___
12. 1, 7, 12, ___
13. 1, 8, 9, ___
14. 1, 8, 10, ___
15. 1, 8, 11, ___
16. 1, 8, 12, ___
17. 1, 9, 10, ___
18. 1, 9, 11, ___
19. 1, 10, 11, ___
20. 2, 3, 13, ___
21. 2, 3, 14, ___
22. 2, 4, 12, ___

23. 2, 4, 13, ___
24. 2, 5, 11, ___
25. 2, 5, 12, ___
26. 2, 5, 13, ___
27. 2, 6, 10, ___
28. 2, 6, 11, ___
29. 2, 6, 12, ___
30. 2, 7, 9, ___
31. 2, 7, 10, ___
32. 2, 7, 11, ___
33. 2, 7, 12, ___
34. 2, 8, 9, ___
35. 2, 8, 10, ___
36. 2, 8, 11, ___
37. 2, 9, 10, ___
38. 2, 9, 11, ___
39. 3, 4, 11, ___
40. 3, 4, 12, ___
41. 3, 4, 13, ___
42. 3, 5, 10, ___
43. 3, 5, 11, ___
44. 3, 5, 12, ___

45. 3, 6, 9, ___
46. 3, 6, 10, ___
47. 3, 6, 11, ___
48. 3, 6, 12, ___
49. 3, 7, 8, ___
50. 3, 7, 9, ___
51. 3, 7, 10, ___
52. 3, 7, 11, ___
53. 3, 8, 9, ___
54. 3, 8, 10, ___
55. 3, 8, 11, ___
56. 3, 9, 10, ___
57. 4, 5, 9, ___
58. 4, 5, 10, ___
59. 4, 5, 11, ___
60. 4, 5, 12, ___
61. 4, 6, 8, ___
62. 4, 6, 9, ___
63. 4, 6, 10, ___
64. 4, 6, 11, ___
65. 4, 7, 8, ___
66. 4, 7, 9, ___

67. 4, 7, 10, ___
68. 4, 7, 11, ___
69. 4, 8, 9, ___
70. 4, 8, 10, ___
71. 4, 9, 10, ___
72. 5, 6, 7, ___
73. 5, 6, 8, ___
74. 5, 6, 9, ___
75. 5, 6, 10, ___
76. 5, 6, 11, ___
77. 5, 7, 8, ___
78. 5, 7, 9, ___
79. 5, 7, 10, ___
80. 5, 8, 9, ___
81. 5, 8, 10, ___
82. 6, 7, 8, ___
83. 6, 7, 9, ___
84. 6, 7, 10, ___
85. 6, 8, 9, ___
86. 7, 8, 9, ___

Egyptian and Greek Number Systems

Ancient Egyptian Numbers

The ancient Egyptians used picture symbols called
hieroglyphs for numerals: / = stick = 1, ∩ = heelbone = 10,
𝕲 = coil of rope = 100, 𝔏 = lotus flower = 1,000.
Each numeral was like an addition algorithm.

The numeral 6,425 was written by the ancient Egyptians as:

Write these Hindu Arabic numerals using ancient Egyptian numerals.

1. 3,425 = _____

2. 6,715 = _____

3. 4,529 = _____

4. 5,826 = _____

5. 4,106 = _____

Note that the ancient Egyptians did not have a symbol for zero.

It is the zero in our system that allows us to have numbers keep their place in a column.

Now you have written some numbers using ancient Egyptian numerals, write 9,999 and, in a sentence
or two, tell why our system is a more efficient way of writing numbers.

9,999 = _____

_____

Why is our system more efficient? _____

_____

_____

Ancient Greek Numerals

The system of writing numerals in ancient Greece was more efficient than that of ancient Egypt because
it included a symbol for 5. Some examples of Greek numbers are:

| = 1 ||| = 3   Γ = 5   Γ|||| = 9   △ = 10   △△Γ| = 26   H = 100
HH△△△Γ||| = 238   X = 1,000   XXHHH△△△| = 2,331

Write these Hindu-Arabic numerals using ancient Greek numerals.
Remember that, like the system of ancient Egypt, this system depended on addition.

---

1. 3,247 = _____

2. 4,319 = _____

3. 5,426 = _____

4. 2,308 = _____

5. 1,234 = _____

Old Chinese Numerals

Numerals are the signs we make to stand for numbers.
The numerals below are from ancient China.

| | 1 | 2 | 3 | 4 | 5 | 6 | 7 | 8 | 9 | 10 | 100 |

Follow the example and write these numbers in Chinese numerals.

642	283	461	512	789	842	678	714	913

312	697	123	826	486	931	452	456	194

Ancient Chinese numerals did not use a symbol for zero. Follow the examples.

350	208	207	540	801	910	709	390	780

360	603	720	805	210	405	904	640	180

Math Words on Holiday

Everyone needs a holiday. The math words in the list have gone to new settings in the sentences below. Put them in their correct locations and then find them in the puzzle. Words read letter to letter in any direction except diagonally. Color answer blocks that connect to one another in different colors.

T	I	A	P	L	U	S	F	O	E	N
E	M	D	B	E	R	S	R	U	T	I
S	I	D	M	U	N	R	U	I	R	N
I	T	A	R	E	R	E	L	A	E	Y
O	N	U	Q	D	I	V	E	N	R	L
T	E	R	S	I	S	I	L	G	U	P
R	A	H	F	O	N	M	E	A	S	I
Q	U	A	L	C	I	R	C	L	E	T
E	E	E	L	E	E	K	A	T	A	L
H	R	V	T	E	A	W	A	E	N	U
T	N	E	U	N	I	M	Y	L	G	M

division   triangle
Times   number
addition   ruler
circle
multiply
angle
minute
Measure
half
nine
square
plus fours

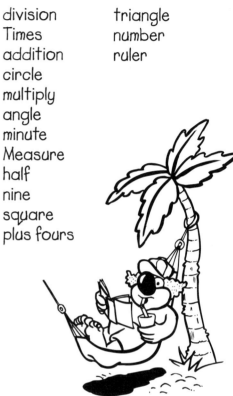

1. Mary has a lovely _____ of friends.

2. "Your _____ is up," said the policeman to the criminal as he was led off to prison.

3. A germ is a _____ living organism.

4. The London _____ is a famous newspaper.

5. Muhammed Ali was a boxing champion in the heavyweight _____ .

6. Rabbits can _____ very quickly.

7. John plays the _____ in the orchestra.

8. The flying buttress was a charming _____ to Carol's house.

9. You should have three _____ meals a day.

10. Many people like to _____ for trout in Colorado's rivers.

11. Golfers used to wear unusual trousers called _____ _____ .

12. The _____-back is a key player on a football team.

13. "_____ for Measure" is a play by William Shakespeare.

14. King Alfred the Great was a wise _____ of England.

15. Someone who is lavishly dressed is said to be "dressed to the _____s".

What's My Number?

Choose from the numbers below to complete each sentence.

1. Many people enjoy _____ pin bowling.

2. The city of Rome was built on _____ hills.

3. There are _____ sides to a triangle.

4. To be elaborately dressed is to be "dressed to the _____s".

5. _____ is said to be company while _____ is said to be a crowd.

6. The Colossus of Rhodes was one of the _____ Wonders of the World.

7. A small, quiet town is sometimes called a _____-horse town.

8. A _____-poster is a bed with curtains around it.

9. There are _____ pennies in a dime.

10. The _____ Bears were very fond of porridge.

11. _____ is the name of a card game.

12. There are said to be _____ Deadly Sins.

13. A _____ o'clock shadow appears on a man with a heavy beard.

14. A pilot always aims for a _____-point landing.

15. There are _____ months in a year.

16. A cat is said to have _____ lives.

17. A _____-wheel drive car is necessary when driving over very rough country.

18. _____ blind mice had their tails cut off by a farmer's wife.

19. A quarter is the same as _____ cents.

20. A _____-leaf clover is said to bring good luck.

21. A person who is _____-faced cannot be trusted.

22. The _____ Little Pigs were almost made into bacon burgers by a wolf.

23. At a picnic you might compete in a _____-legged race.

(ten) (two) (two) (five hundred) (three) (three) (four) (nine) (one) (ten)

(five) (two) (seven) (seven) ( ) (three) (six) (four) (two) (twelve)

(three) (four) (twenty) (three) (seven) (three) (nine) (three)

Polygons and Diagonals

You can make interesting patterns in polygons by drawing in the diagonals.

The first polygon is called a pentagon. "Penta" means five in the language of ancient Greece.

How many other words can you list with "penta" in them that have something to do with five?

_____   _____

_____   _____

_____   _____

This polygon is called a pentagon.
Rule these diagonals in the pentagon:
AC, AD, BD, BE, CE.

A pentagon has:

_____ sides,

_____ angles, and

_____ diagonals.

This polygon is called a hexagon.

Rule these diagonals on the hexagon:
AC, AD, AE, BD, BE, BF, CE, CF, DF.

A hexagon has:

_____ sides,

_____ angles, and

_____ diagonals.

This polygon is called an octagon.
Rule these diagonals on the octagon:
AC, AD, AE, AF, AG, BD, BE, BF, BG, BH,
CE, CF, CG, CH, DF, DG, DH, EG, EH, FH.

An octagon has

_____ sides,

_____ angles, and

_____ diagonals.

Can you find the relationship between the number of sides a polygon has and its number of diagonals? Ask your teacher for clues.

Amazing Numbers

Mathematics really is amazing. The number 142,857 is amazing. Do the multiplications below and you will see why.

1. 1 4 2 , 8 5 7	2. 1 4 2 , 8 5 7	3. 1 4 2 , 8 5 7	4. 1 4 2 , 8 5 7	5. 1 4 2 , 8 5 7
x 2	x 3	x 4	x 5	x 6

Now multiply it by 7.

6. 1 4 2 , 8 5 7
x   7

This is an amazing number. Write a sentence telling why you think it is so special.

_____

_____

_____

The Square Pattern

$1^2 = 1 \times 1 = 1 = 1$

$2^2 = 2 \times 2 = 4 = 1 + 3$

$3^2 = 3 \times 3 = 9 = 1 + 3 + 5$

$4^2 = 4 \times 4 = 16 = 1 + 3 + 5 + 7$

$5^2 = 5 \times 5 = 25 = $ ___ + ___ + ___ + ___ + ___

$6^2 = 6 \times 6 = 36 = $ ___ + ___ + ___ + ___ + ___ + ___

$7^2 = 7 \times 7 = 49 = $ ___ + ___ + ___ + ___ + ___ + ___ + ___

$8^2 = 8 \times 8 = 64 = $ ___ + ___ + ___ + ___ + ___ + ___ + ___ + ___

$9^2 = 9 \times 9 = 81 = $ ___ + ___ + ___ + ___ + ___ + ___ + ___ + ___ + ___

$10^2 = 10 \times 10 = 100 = $ ___ + ___ + ___ + ___ + ___ + ___ + ___ + ___ + ___ + ___

When we square a number we multiply it by itself. You can check your answer using the pattern below. Check the answers for 1 to 4 then extend the pattern.

The Cube Pattern

$1^3 = 1 \times 1 \times 1 = 1 = 1$

$2^3 = 2 \times 2 \times 2 = 8 = 3 + 5$

$3^3 = 3 \times 3 \times 3 = 27 = 7 + 9 + 11$

$4^3 = 4 \times 4 \times 4 = 64 = 13 + 15 + 17 + 19$

$5^3 = 5 \times 5 \times 5 = 125 = $ ___ + ___ + ___ + ___ + ___

$6^3 = 6 \times 6 \times 6 = 216 = $ ___ + ___ + ___ + ___ + ___ + ___

$7^3 = 7 \times 7 \times 7 = 343 = $ ___ + ___ + ___ + ___ + ___ + ___ + ___

$8^3 = 8 \times 8 \times 8 = 512 = $ ___ + ___ + ___ + ___ + ___ + ___ + ___ + ___

$9^3 = 9 \times 9 \times 9 = 729 = $ ___ + ___ + ___ + ___ + ___ + ___ + ___ + ___ + ___

$10^3 = 10 \times 10 \times 10 = 1,000 = $ ___ + ___ + ___ + ___ + ___ + ___ + ___ + ___ + ___ + ___

When we multiply a number by itself again after squaring we are cubing the number. You can check your answers using the pattern below. Check the answers for 1 to 4 then extend the pattern.

More Amazing Numbers

Amazing Seven

In his play, 'As You Like It', William Shakespeare divides a person's life into intervals of 7 years. He wrote:

Seven years in childhood, sport and play, (7)
Seven years in school from day to day, (14)
Seven years at trade or college life, (21)
Seven years to find a place and wife, (28)
Seven years to pleasure's follies given, (35)
Seven years to business hardly driven, (42)
Seven years for some wild goose chase, (49)
Seven years for wealth, a bootless race, (56)
Seven years of hoarding for your heir, (63)
Seven years in weakness spent in care, (70)
And then you die and go — you know not where.

Use your own words to describe what Shakespeare meant in each stage.

_____

_____

_____

_____

_____

_____

_____

_____

_____

_____

_____

_____

_____

_____

Do the multiplications below to discover more about the amazing number seven.

1. 15,873
    x   7
    _____

    _____

2. 31,746
    x   7
    _____

    _____

3. 47,619
    x   7
    _____

    _____

4. 63,492
    x   7
    _____

    _____

5. 79,365
    x   7
    _____

    _____

6. 95,238
    x   7
    _____

    _____

7. 111,111
    x   7
    _____

    _____

8. 126,984
    x   7
    _____

    _____

9. 142,857
    x   7
    _____

    _____

Acrostics

An acrostic is a type of poem in which the first letters of each line form a word. The content of the poem is usually related to the word. Write your own acrostic about a number.

Seven days in a week.

Every rainbow has seven colors.

VII makes a Roman seven.

Everyone has heard of the Seven Wonders of the World.

Netball teams have seven players.

High-Interest Activities in Mathematics ● World Teachers Press ● Page 31

Still More Amazing Numbers

Another Amazing Number

Do the multiplication algorithms below and find out why 76,923 is an amazing number.

1. 7 6 9 2 3   2. 7 6 9 2 3   3. 7 6 9 2 3   4. 7 6 9 2 3   5. 7 6 9 2 3
       x   2   x   5   x   7   x   8   x   1 1

    _____   _____   _____   _____   _____

    _____   _____   _____   _____   _____

                                                                                    _____

Now do the multiplications below to reveal a new pattern for 76,923.

1. 7 6 9 2 3   2. 7 6 9 2 3   3. 7 6 9 2 3   4. 7 6 9 2 3   5. 7 6 9 2 3
       x   3   x   4   x   9   x   1 0   x   1 2

    _____   _____   _____   _____   _____

    _____   _____   _____   _____   _____

                                                                                    _____

                                                                                    _____

Numbers In Sequence

Find the answers to these number sentences. Notice that the numbers 1 through to 9 are used in sequence.

This time the numbers are reversed 9 through to 1.

1. $1 + 2 + 3 + 4 + 5 + 6 + 7 + (8 \times 9) =$ _____ $98 - 76 + 54 + 3 + 21 =$ _____

2. $123 - 45 - 67 + 89 =$ _____

3. $12 + 3 - 4 + 5 + 67 + 8 + 9 =$ _____

Amazing Squares

$13^2 =$ _____   What is unusual about these square numbers?

$31^2 =$ _____   _____

What number am I?
I am less than 10.
I am the only number that gives a bigger answer when you add me to myself than when you multiply me by myself.

I am ____ .

What number am I?
I am less than 10.
I give the same answer when added to myself as when multiplied by myself.

I am ____ .

What number am I?
I am the only number with the same number of letters in my name as myself.

I am written _____ .

My numeral is ____ .

What number am I?
If you wrote the numbers 1 to 10 in words then put them in alphabetical order, I would come first.

I am ____ .

 What is triskaidekaphobia? _____

_____

Lightning Multiplication

If two two-digit numbers have the same number in the tens column and their units columns added together equal ten, you can do a "lightning" calculation to find their product.

Example: 36 x 34

Step # 1

Multiply the units column .... 6 x 4 = 24

Write this as the units and tens part of the answer.

Step # 2

Increase one of the tens column numbers by one

and then multiply it by the other .... 3 x 4 = 12

Step # 3

Write the Step 2 answer in front of the Step 1 answer 1,224

Check your answer either using long multiplication or a calculator.

When your first number is a single digit number write this with a 0 in the tens column in your answer.

Example: 41 x 49 = ?

\# 1   1 x 9 = 9 (Write 09)

\# 2   4 x 5 = 20

\# 3   Answer = 2,009

Now it's your turn. Work out your answers step by step then check them.

1. 14 x 16	2. 29 x 21	3. 35 x 35	4. 43 x 47
\# 1 _____	\# 1 _____	\# 1 _____	\# 1 _____
\# 2 _____	\# 2 _____	\# 2 _____	\# 2 _____
\# 3 _____	\# 3 _____	\# 3 _____	\# 3 _____
Check _____	Check _____	Check _____	Check _____

5. 52 x 58	6. 67 x 63	7. 81 x 89	8. 98 x 92
\# 1 _____	\# 1 _____	\# 1 _____	\# 1 _____
\# 2 _____	\# 2 _____	\# 2 _____	\# 2 _____
\# 3 _____	\# 3 _____	\# 3 _____	\# 3 _____
Check _____	Check _____	Check _____	Check _____

Now that you are good at these calculations, you will be able to do these in "lightning" time.

1. 11 x 19 = _____   2. 22 x 28 = _____   3. 37 x 33 = _____

4. 48 x 42 = _____   5. 53 x 57 = _____   6. 64 x 66 = _____

7. 95 x 95 = _____   8. 62 x 68 = _____   9. 86 x 84 = _____

This method works with three-digit numbers as well. Do these on paper.

Example: 164 x 166 = ?

\# 1 4 x 6 = 24

\# 2 16 x 17 = 272

\# 3 Answer = 27,224

1. 111 x 119 = _____   2. 128 x 122 = _____

3. 134 x 136 = _____   4. 145 x 145 = _____

5. 176 x 174 = _____   6. 487 x 483 = _____

Which Day ?

No doubt, you know the date of your birthday. But do you know the exact day of the week when you were born? Using the tables and method below you can find out which day it was on any given date from the beginning of the Christian era (i.e., the years since Christ's birth) up to the year 3000 AD.

Table 1: The Table for the Months

Month	Ratio	Month	Ratio
January	3	July	2
February	6	August	5
March	6	September	1
April	2	October	3
May	4	November	6
June	0	December	1

Table 2: The Century Table

00's	Ratio	00's	Ratio
00s	2	1400s	2
100s	1	1500s	1
200s	0	1600s	4
300s	6	1700s	2
400s	5	1800s	0
500s	4	1900s	5
600s	3	2000s	4
700s	2	2100s	2
800s	1	2200s	0
900s	0	2300s	5
1000s	6	2400s	4
1100s	5	2500s	2
1200s	4	2600s	0
1300s	3	2700s	5

Table 3: Table of Days

Day	#	Day	#
Saturday	0	Wednesday	4
Sunday	1	Thursday	5
Monday	2	Friday	6
Tuesday	3		

Method:

Select a date, for example, April 25, 1915.

Step #1	Write the last 2 digits of the year.	
	i.e. The last two digits in 1915 are 15	15
Step #2	Divide this number by 4 and ignore any remainder you get in your answer.	
	i.e. 15 divided by 4 = 3 (the remainder is 3 but ignore it)	
	Add your answer to the number already written.	3
Step #3	Add the day of the month i.e., 25	25
Step #4	Add the ratio number for the month from Table 1.	2
Step #5	Add the ratio number for the century from Table 2.	
	i.e. 1900s = 5	5
Step #6	The total of steps 1 to 5 = 50	50
	Divide this total by 7. 50 ÷ 7 = 7 remainder 1	
	Check this remainder with its day in table 3.	
	1 means Sunday. So April 25, 1915 was a Sunday.	

Positions on a map are often named with a grid reference.
Read the questions below. Use the grid coordinates given to find the correct letter. Color the letter on the grid using the color given in the answer boxes. Color any leftover boxes with a vowel in them yellow and leftover boxes with a consonant in them light blue.

	A	B	C	D	E	F	G	H
8	M	N	L	S	E	O	H	J
7	S	T	N	A	E	L	F	G
6	R	B	O	I	O	E	D	C
5	G	O	I	M	H	I	D	B
4	H	U	M	G	O	N	Y	Z
3	K	A	V	G	O	I	U	Y
2	L	E	N	Q	N	R	T	X
1	M	N	A	P	S	S	V	W

How do you pronounce VOLIX?

C3	B5	C8	G3	D5	B2
BLACK	RED	GREEN	RED	RED	RED

C7	C5	C2	F6
GREEN	RED	BLACK	GREEN

What is grey and has a trunk?

B3		C4	C6	B4	D8	E8
RED		RED	GREEN	RED	GREEN	GREEN

D4	E3	F3	F4	D3		F8	E2
RED	BLACK	RED	RED	RED		GREEN	BLACK

E5	E4	F7	F5	G5	C1	G4	E1
RED	RED	GREEN	RED	RED	BLACK	RED	BLACK

The Lost Treasure of Captain Bluerinsebeard

The race is on to find the lost treasure of Captain Bluerinsebeard, the ferocious pirate. Starting at X each time, color the paths taken by each adventurer. Some of the paths will overlap.

1. Jim went 4 spaces right, 1 space down, 4 spaces right, 3 spaces down, 1 space right then 2 spaces down.
2. Butch Dog went 3 spaces down, 2 spaces right, 3 spaces down, 2 spaces left, 1 space down, 6 spaces right, 2 spaces down, 2 spaces right then 1 space up.
3. Sir Laurence Stick Insect led a party from the Royal Society. They went 1 space down, 3 spaces right, 3 spaces down, 2 spaces right, 6 spaces down, 3 spaces left then 1 space up.
4. Bruce went 1 space right, 2 spaces down, 6 spaces right, 8 spaces down then 2 spaces right.

Each adventurer found a treasure of some sort at the end of their journey.
List what they found:

Jim _____ Butch _____

Sir Laurence _____ Bruce _____

Who did the following things to find the Treasure?

Who swam Slime Creek? _____

Who tiptoed through the soldier crab colony? _____

Write your own directions to the treasure starting from "X".

_____

Plot each point on the grid below. Join each plotted point in order as you are doing this.
The first three points have already been plotted for you. Cross out points from the coordinates list as you plot them.

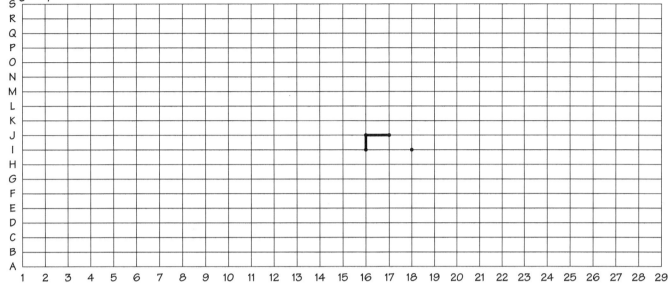

Coordinates

The grid shows a _____

1. 17J	2. 16J	3. 16I	4. 18I	5. 18K	6. 15K	7. 15H
8. 19H	9. 19L	10. 14L	11. 14G	12. 20G	13. 20M	14. 13M
15. 13F	16. 21F	17. 21N	18. 12N	19. 12E	20. 22E	21. 23F
22. 23N	23. 21O	24. 12O	25. 10M	26. 10F	27. 7F	28. 7H
29. 5H	30. 4G	31. 4F	32. 6E	33. 7C	34. 29C	35. 23E
36. 22E						

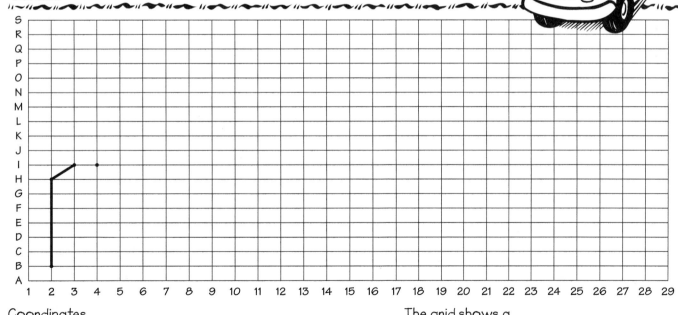

Coordinates

The grid shows a _____

1. 2B	2. 2H	3. 3I	4. 4I	5. 4J	6. 5I	7. 5J
8. 6I	9. 6J	10. 7I	11. 7J	12. 8I	13. 8J	14. 9I
15. 9J	16. 10I	17. 10J	18. 11I	19. 13I	20. 14R	21. 15R
22. 16I	23. 19I	24. 20R	25. 21R	26. 22I	27. 25I	28. 25H
29. 28H	30. 28B	31. 2B				

Following Directions – Instructions

Follow the directions to make a picture on graph paper. Place a dot at the beginning point and follow the directions from there. Place a dot after each full direction given and rule a line from the last point to it.

A. Start at point I28

1. E1	2. S1, E1	3. S1	4. S1, W1	5. S7, W2	6. S1, E1
7. N1, E2	8. N1, E6	9. S3, E2	10. N1, W2	11. S3, E2	12. N1, W2
13. S3, E2	14. N1, W2	15. S3, E2	16. N1, W4	17. W4	18. S8
19. S1, E1	20. W4	21. N1, E2	22. N8	23. N1, W1	24. W4
25. N6, E1	26. N7, E3	27. N1, W1	28. W2	29. N1, E2	30. N1, E1

B. Start at point D24

1. S2, E2	2. N1, E1	3. E3	4. S2, E2	5. E1	6. S1, E1
7. S1, W1	8. E2	9. S2, E3	10. S2, W1	11. S2	12. S2, W3
13. S2, W2	14. W2	15. S1, E1	16. S1, W1	17. S4, W1	18. S1
19. N1, W1	20. N10	21. N1, W2	22. N3, W2	23. N2	24. N2, E1
25. N2, W2					

C. Start at point A21

1. S1, E4	2. S5, E1	3. S2, W1	4. S6, E3	5. N3, W1	6. S3, E2
7. S1	8. S2, E6	9. S1, E2	10. N1, W1	11. N1	12. W1
13. N2	14. W1	15. S1, W1	16. W1	17. N2, W1	18. N2, E2
19. E2	20. S2, E2	21. N3, W1	22. N1, E1	23. N4, E1	24. N1
25. S1, W1	26. N3, E1	27. N2, W2	28. S1	29. N1, W2	30. S4, E1
31. N1, W3	32. N3	33. N1, W1	34. S1, W2	35. N4, W5	36. S2, W1
37. S1, W1	38. S1, E1	39. W2			

D. Start at point A5

1. N4	2. E2	3. N7, W1	4. E1	5. S7, E1	6. E1
7. S1	8. E2	9. N15	10. E2	11. N3, W2	12. N3, E2
13. S2, E2	14. S4, W2	15. N3, W1	16. N1, E1	17. S1, E1	18. S3, W1
19. E2, N1	20. S16	21. E4	22. N2, E2	23. S2	24. S3, W1
25. W15					

E. Start at point G1

1. N1, W4	2. N1, W1	3. N24	4. N1, E1	5. N1, E4	6. S4
7. W1	8. S10	9. E4	10. N1	11. E1	12. S3
13. E3	14. S1	15. E1	16. S1	17. W1	18. S1
19. W3	20. S4	21. W5	22. S3	23. E1	24. S2

F. Start at point A3

1. S1, E2	2. E14	3. N4, E2	4. N8	
5. W3	6. S1	7. E2	8. S7	
9. S3, W2	10. W14	11. N3, E3	12. S1, E1	
13. E5	14. N1, E2	15. N2, E2	16. N10	
17. N2, W3	18. N2, E2	19. N2	20. N2, W2	
21. N3, W1	22. S3, W1	23. W3	24. N3, W1	
25. S3, W1	26. S2, W2	27. S2	28. S2, E2	
29. S2, W3	30. S10	31. S2, E2	32. S3, W3	

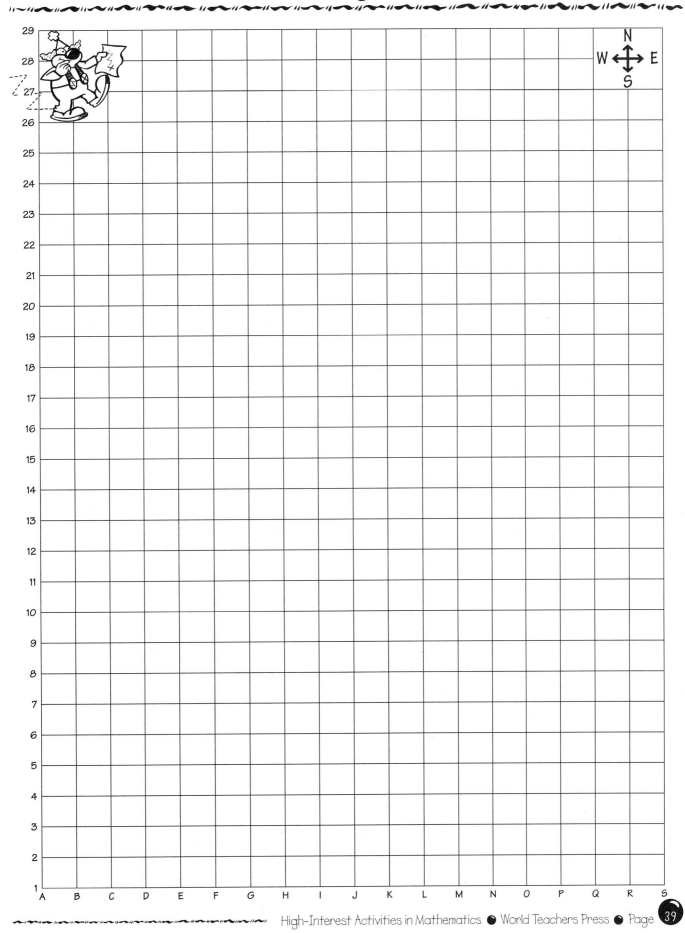

Answers

Words in order are: Greece, great, found, baths, Hiero, goldsmith, king, with, quite, given, melted, weighed, volume, find, foot, overflowed, found, displaced, volume, more, death.

Picture shows a city skyline.

Picture shows a truck.

Picture shows a lighthouse.

1. 80	2. 190	3. 100	4. 90	5. 30
6. 200	7. 230	8. 280	9. 300	10. 60
11. 290	12. 210	13. 110	14. 140	15. 220
16. 40	17. 240	18. 70	19. 120	20. 150
21. 170	22. 50	23. 250	24. 180	25. 130
26. 260	27. 160	28. 270	29. 310	30. 80

Picture shows a clown in a car.

Al rides 320 m to school every mornings.

1. 30¢	2. 35¢	3. 35¢	4. 50¢	5. 70¢
6. 40¢	7. 60¢	8. 50¢	9. 55¢	10. 45¢
11. 60¢	12. 50¢	13. 50¢	14. 45¢	15. 50¢
16. 40¢	17. 60¢	18. 45¢	19. 60¢	20. 45¢
21. 50¢	22. 40¢	23. 65¢	24. 60¢	25. 35¢

The ships of the first fleet are: Sirius, Supply, Alexander, Charlotte, Friendship, Lady Penrhyn, Prince of Wales, Scarborough, Borrowdale, Fishburn, Golden Grove.

1. Midnite	2. bushranger	3. Khat
4. Gyp	5. Red Ned	6. Major
7. Dora	8. O'Grady	

1. Apollo	2. Eleven	3. Voyager
4. station	5. Freedom	

Answers in order are: Black Beauty, Anna Sewell, died, sympathy, suffering.

1. eat	2. Mom	3. Dad
4. gas	5. car	6. bodies
7. food	8. sugar	9. salt
10. fat		

Answers in order are: JRR Tolkien, The Hobbit, adventure, Bilbo Baggins.

Answers in order are: rat, mole, toad, weasels, ferrets

Teacher check.

Teacher check.

1.

□	36	42	58	156	100	171	52	76	118
△	3	6	7	12	8	12	4	8	10
○	9	2	3	4	12	9	12	4	6

2.

▽	6	14	11	23	1	1	28	0	38	26	1	25	11	5
	3	6	5	12	10	1	7	0	11	8	2	9	4	5
	6	10	9	25	39	3	0	0	6	6	7	11	5	15

3.

☿	6	2	1	3	0	19	0	50	2	10	9	8	1	5
	7	10	20	9	14	15	12	100	17	13	11	16	8	5
	6	13	24	11	19	1	17	55	20	8	7	13	12	5

4.

◉	1	9	7	9	2	4	1	6	5	0	4	6	12	6
○	3	6	7	12	8	12	4	8	10	0	8	10	8	12
●	9	2	3	4	12	9	12	4	6	6	6	6	5	2	6

5.

▯	10	27	19	20	26	15	19	27	0	10	11	8	10	9
▲	8	9	7	10	6	7	5	11	4	12	5	8	6	7
◑	3	11	8	7	12	6	9	10	0	1	5	2	4	3

6.

✕	0	7	5	1	3	0	3	0	9	1	2	15	7	12
	3	6	8	5	10	2	12	7	5	1	11	9	4	12
▪	6	5	11	9	17	4	21	14	1	1	20	3	1	12

1.

X	3	5	10	12	2	1	$\frac{1}{2}$	4	30	6	9
Y	10	26	101	145	5	2	$1\frac{1}{2}$	17	901	37	82

2.

A	2	7	3	1	3	5	7	9	2	1	3	6	2	5	5
B	3	4	6	7	2	8	6	8	11	0	5	10	9	$\frac{1}{2}$	7
C	13	65	45	50	13	89	85	145	125	1	34	136	85	$25\frac{1}{4}$	74

3.

N	3	6	2	1	4	2	5	6	2	3	3	5	5	7	5
Q	5	4	9	3	6	7	8	7	10	4	8	5	8	10	11
D	21	24	31	11	26	25	34	33	34	18	30	25	34	44	43

4.

B	9	8	2	7	8	5	2	12	7	6	10	11	1	5
P	2	6	5	6	2	10	4	4	18	14	6	8	28	3	0
F	50	36	2	30	44	10	34	4	36	14	24	44	10	0	30

5.

X	6	8	4	12	22	14	8	10	30	2	5	3	17	3	$\frac{1}{4}$
Y	7	5	9	4	2	1	4	3	6	8	7	6	3	1	1
Z	10	9	11	8	12	11	7	11	23	8	$8\frac{1}{2}$	$4\frac{1}{2}$	$9\frac{1}{2}$	$2\frac{1}{2}$	$8\frac{1}{8}$

6.

B	6	9	3	8	4	7	5	10	12	1	4	11	5	5	4
C	4	10	16	22	28	8	14	12	16	50	3	15	8	7	$\frac{1}{2}$
D	38	86	17	75	30	53	32	106	152	26	$17\frac{1}{2}$	$128\frac{1}{2}$	29	$28\frac{1}{2}$	$16\frac{1}{4}$

7.

P	7	9	8	6	5	3	6	10	12	11	13	1	0	7	8
Q	26	19	9	12	7	14	9	5	6	1	14	7	$\frac{1}{2}$	$5\frac{1}{2}$	$1\frac{1}{2}$
R	0	13	20	11	13	0	12	30	35	37	30	1	$4\frac{1}{2}$	$20\frac{1}{2}$	$27\frac{1}{2}$

Teacher check.

1. his	2. goose	3. sell
4. his	5. geese	6. eggs
7. soil	8. shoe	9. bees
10. log	11. he	12. legs

13. silos   14. hellish   15. high
16. globes   17. gosh   18. bells
19. big   20. bill   21. ibis
22. gobble   23. heel   24. shells
25. loose   26. soil   27. sell
28. shells   29. glee   30. shoosh
31. hobble   32. eels

Magic Squares . . . . page 23

1. (sum 12)

3	8	1
2	4	6
7	0	5

2. (sum 30)

9	14	7
8	10	12
13	6	11

3. (sum 39)

14	9	16
15	13	11
10	17	12

4. (sum 12)

1	8	3
6	4	2
5	0	7

5. (sum 15)

2	9	4
7	5	3
6	1	8

6. (sum 39)

16	11	12
9	13	17
14	15	10

7. (sum 42)

15	10	17
16	14	12
11	18	13

8. (sum 18)

3	10	5
8	6	4
7	2	9

9. (sum 33)

13	3	17
15	11	7
5	19	9

10. (sum 30)

8	18	4
6	10	14
16	2	12

11. (sum 60)

22	15	23
21	20	19
17	25	18

12. (sum 33)

8	15	10
13	11	9
12	7	14

13. (sum 54)

15	22	17
20	18	16
19	14	21

14. (sum 54)

21	16	17
14	18	22
19	20	15

15. (sum 36)

13	8	15
14	12	10
9	16	11

Diabolical! . . . . page 24

1. 16	2. 16	3. 17	4. 15	5. 16
6. 15	7. 16	8. 15	9. 14	10. 16
11. 15	12. 14	13. 16	14. 15	15. 14
16. 13	17. 14	18. 13	19. 12	20. 16
21. 15	22. 16	23. 15	24. 16	25. 15
26. 14	27. 16	28. 15	29. 14	30. 16
31. 15	32. 14	33. 13	34. 15	35. 14
36. 13	37. 13	38. 12	39. 16	40. 15
41. 14	42. 16	43. 15	44. 14	45. 16
46. 15	47. 15	48. 13	49. 16	50. 15
51. 14	52. 13	53. 14	54. 13	55. 12
56. 12	57. 16	58. 15	59. 14	60. 13
61. 16	62. 15	63. 14	64. 13	65. 15
66. 14	67. 13	68. 12	69. 13	70. 12
71. 11	72. 16	73. 15	74. 14	75. 13
76. 12	77. 14	78. 13	79. 12	80. 12
81. 11	82. 13	83. 12	84. 11	85. 11
86. 10				

Egyptian and Greek Number Systems . . . . page 25

Ancient Egyptian Numerals:

1.

2.

3.

4.

5.

9 999 =

Our number system is more efficient because it uses fewer numerals. In this example 36 numerals have to be written using the Egyptian system.

Ancient Greek Numerals

1. ΧΧΧΗΗΔΔΔΓΙΙ

2. ΧΧΧΧΗΗΗΔΓΙΙΙΙ

3. ΧΧΧΧΧΗΗΗΗΔΔΓΙ

4. ΧΧΗΗΗΓΙΙΙ

5. ΧΗΗΔΔΔΙΙΙΙ

Old Chinese Numerals . . . . page 26

Answers

Maths Words on Holiday .... page 27

1. circle
2. number
3. minute
4. Times
5. division
6. multiply
7. triangle
8. addition
9. square
10. angle
11. plus fours
12. half
13. Measure   14. ruler   15. nine

What's My Number? .... page 28

1. hundreds and thousands
2. ten
3. seven
4. three
5. nine
6. Two, three
7. Seven
8. one
9. four
10. Ten
11. three
12. Five hundred
13. Seven
14. five
15. three
16. twelve
17. nine
18. four
19. Three
20. twenty-five
21. four
22. two
23. Three
24. three

Polygons and Diagonals .... page 29

Words with 'penta':

pentacle, pentad, pentagram, pentahedron, pentameter, pentane, pentangle, pentangle, pentathlon

Pentagon = 5 sides, 5 angles, 5 diagonals
Hexagon = 6 sides, 6 angles, 9 diagonals
Octagon = 8 sides, 8 angles, 20 diagonals

Ratio of diagonals to sides:
quadrilateral = 2 diagonals = # of sides x 0.5
pentagon = 5 diagonals = # of sides x 1
hexagon = 5 diagonals = # of sides x 1.5
heptagon = 5 diagonals = # of sides x 2
octagon = 5 diagonals = # of sides x 2.5
nonagon = 5 diagonals = # of sides x 3
decagon = 5 diagonals = # of sides x 3.5

Amazing Numbers .... page 30

1. 285,714
2. 428,571
3. 571,428
4. 714,285
5. 857,142
6. 999,999

If you start at the number 1 in each answer and read left to right, you will find the number 142,857.

Square Pattern
Add the next odd number in each group to make the next square number.

Cube Pattern
Continue adding the odd numbers in series and extending each addition by another addend.

More Amazing Numbers .... page 31

1. 111,111
2. 222,222
3. 333,333
4. 444,444
5. 555,555
6. 666,666
7. 777,777
8. 888,888
9. 999,999

Still More Amazing Numbers .... page 32

Another Amazing Number
1. 153,846
2. 384,615
3. 538,461
4. 615,384
5. 846,153

1. 230,769
2. 307,692
3. 692,307
4. 769,230
5. 923,076

Still More Amazing Numbers (continued) ...... page 32

Numbers In Sequence
All number sentences equal 100.

Amazing Squares
$13^2 = 169$, $31^2 = 961$
The numbers and their squares are the reverse of one another. This is the only pair of numbers with these properties.

What Number am I?
1   2   four, 4   8

Triskaidekaphobia is a fear of the number 13.

Lightning Multiplication .... page 33

Step-by-step Answers
1. 224
2. 609
3. 1,225
4. 2,021
5. 3,016
6. 4,221
7. 7,209
8. 9,016

Quick Answers
1. 209
2. 616
3. 1,221
4. 2,016
5. 3,021
6. 4,224
7. 9,025
8. 4,216
9. 7,224

Three Digit Numeral Answers
1. 13,209
2. 15,616
3. 18,224
4. 21,025
5. 30,624
6. 235,221

Grid Coordinates .... page 35

Q: How do you pronounce volix?
A: Volume Nine
Q: What is grey and has a trunk?
A: A mouse going on holidays.

The Lost Treasure of Captain Bluerinsebeard .. page 36

Jim – balloons, Sir Laurence – matching tie and socks, Butch – rubber bone, Bruce – treasure

Sir Laurence swam Slime Creek.
Butch tiptoed through the soldier crab colony.

Grid Positions .... page 37

The first grid shows a snail. The second grid shows a factory.

Following Directions .... page 38/39

A. Emu
B. S. America
C. N. America
D. Candle
E. Boat
F. Cat